KINGFISHER
Kingfisher Publications Plc
New Penderel House
283-288 High Holborn
London WC1V 7HZ
www.kingfisherpub.co.uk

First published by
Kingfisher Publications Plc 2001
10 9 8 7 6 5 4 3 2 1

1TR/1200/FR/SC/128JDA

Created and designed by Snapdragon Publishing Limited

A CIP catalogue record for this book is available
in the British Library.

ISBN 0 7534 0558 X

Printed in Hong Kong

Author Janice Lobb
Illustrators Peter Utton and Ann Savage

For Snapdragon
Editorial Director Jackie Fortey
Art Director Chris Legee
Designers Chris Legee and Joy Fitzsimons

For Kingfisher
Series Editor Emma Wild
Series Art Editor Mike Davis
DTP Co-ordinator Nicky Studdart
Production Debbie Otter

Contents

About this book

Ever wondered how a budgie keeps its feathers clean, or why a hamster is soft and furry while a snake is covered with scales? This book shows you all kinds of exciting discoveries you can make about animals, with the help of pets at home or in the classroom. You don't even need to have a pet of your own to join in the fun.

Which?

What?

How?

Where?

Why?

What if?

Hall of Fame

Archie and his friends are here to help you. They are named after famous scientists – apart from Bob the duck, who is a young scientist just like you!

Archie
ARCHIMEDES (287–212BC)
The Greek scientist Archimedes worked out why things float or sink while he was in the bath. According to the story, he was so pleased that he leapt out, shouting 'Eureka!', which means 'I've done it!'

Frank
BENJAMIN FRANKLIN (1706–1790)
This American statesman carried out a famous (but dangerous) experiment in 1752. By flying a kite in a storm, he proved that a flash of lightning was actually electricity. This helped people to protect buildings during storms.

Marie
MARIE CURIE (1867–1934)
Girls did not go to university in Poland, where Marie Curie grew up, so she went to study in Paris, France. She worked on radioactivity and received two Nobel prizes for her discoveries, in 1903 and 1911.

Dot
DOROTHY HODGKIN (1910–1994)
Dorothy Hodgkin was a British scientist who made many important discoveries about molecules and atoms, the tiny particles that make up everything around us. She was given the Nobel prize for Chemistry in 1964.

See for yourself!

1 Read the science facts about animals, then try the 'See for yourself!' experiments to see them in action. In science, experiments try to find or show the answers.

2 Read the instructions for each experiment carefully, making sure you follow the numbered steps in the correct order.

3 Here are some of the things you will need. Have everything ready before you start each experiment.

Toys

Magnifying glass

Catnip

Shoe box

Torch

Balloons

Cloth bag

Plastic box

Bottle

Feathers

Card

Clay

Colouring pencils

Comb

Marbles

Foil

Rubber bands

4 # Safety first! 👋

All the experiments are safe. Just make sure that you tell an adult what you are doing and get their help when you see the red warning button. Remember to always wash your hands after handling your pet.

Amazing facts

WOW!

You'll notice that some words are written in *italics*. You can learn more about them from the glossary at the back of the book. And if you want to find out some amazing facts, look out for the 'Wow!' panels.

Look out for useful tips!

Have fun!

5

How does my cat purr?

Why can cats do no wrong?

Because they are purr-fect!

Sound is a kind of *energy*, which is carried to our ears by movements in the air. When a cat purrs, it puts sound energy into the air by moving part of its throat backwards and forwards quickly. This movement is called a vibration. Every sound you hear is made by something vibrating. It could be a surface, a string, or a column of air. It is difficult to see air moving because it is invisible, but you can see when surfaces and strings vibrate and make the air move.

Making sounds

A cat purrs at the back of its throat, but when it miaows, it uses its vocal cords. Air pushed out from its lungs makes the cords vibrate.

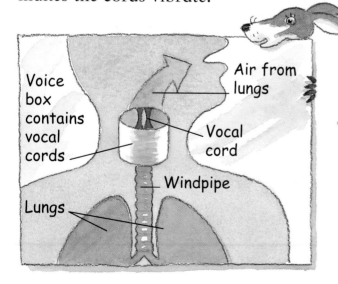

Voice box contains vocal cords

Air from lungs

Vocal cord

Windpipe

Lungs

A cat has a high voice.

A lion has a deep voice.

High notes vibrate in your head. Low ones in your chest.

Small animals have high voices because they have short vocal cords. Large animals have long vocal cords and deep voices.

Human voices sound different when they sing. Air vibrates in the throat, mouth, chest and face too. Try it yourself!

6

See for yourself! ✋

1 All you need to make a drum is a hollow container and a stretchy 'drum skin' (such as a burst rubber balloon) to fix over the open end. Try different sizes for other sounds.

Jar

Plastic tub

Bottle

2 Make a model guitar from a shoe box or ice-cream tub. Get a grown-up to cut two notches in the sides.

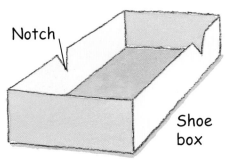

Notch

Shoe box

3 Slot a ruler into the two notches, so that it slants across the box. Put rubber bands around the box, so they rest on the edge of the ruler.

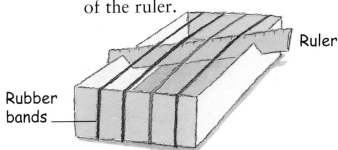

Ruler

Rubber bands

4 Now twang the rubber bands. You can see them vibrate. Long ones make a low sound, short ones make a high sound.

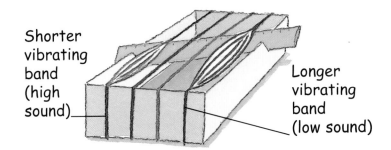

Shorter vibrating band (high sound)

Longer vibrating band (low sound)

WOW! Silence in space!

There is no sound in outer space, because there is no air to carry vibrations. In space, no one can hear you scream!

Noisy pets can annoy your neighbours!

Why does my goldfish look sad?

Because it's feeling gill-ty!

How do fish swim?

When fish swim, they press the sides of their bodies and their flat tails against the water. The water pushes back and they shoot forwards. Most fish are a bit heavier than water, so they have no difficulty in going down to the bottom. To help them float back up, many of them have a bag of air called a *swim bladder*. They fill this with gases taken from their blood, which makes their bodies lighter. They can float in the water at any level without effort.

Streamlined shapes

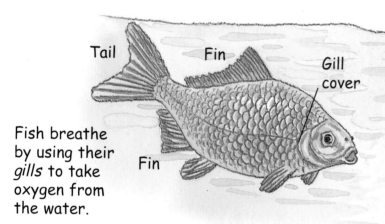

Flying fish

Tail

Fin

Gill cover

Fish breathe by using their *gills* to take oxygen from the water.

Fin

Back fin

Back fin waggles to keep sea horse in position.

To move along, a fish moves its body from side to side. Its *fins* help it to steer in the right direction. A fish can also waggle its fins for smaller movements.

Fish that swim fast have a smooth, streamlined shape. Some fish, such as flying fish, can swim so fast they can leap right out of the water.

Fish with odd shapes, like the sea horse, can't move very fast at all.

See for yourself!

1 To make a diving model, take half a plastic drinking straw. Seal the top with a small piece of modelling clay, then seal the bottom with a large piece.

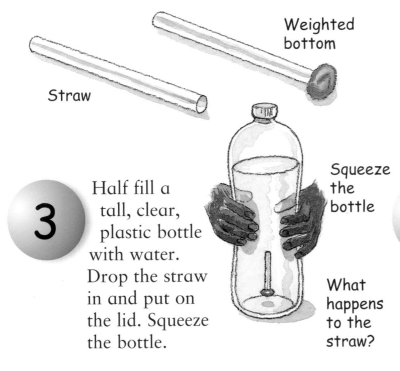

Straw

Weighted bottom

2 Test the straw in a bowl of water. It should float upright below the surface. If it bobs up out of the water, add more clay to make it sink. If it touches the bottom take a bit off.

Surface

Floating straw

3 Half fill a tall, clear, plastic bottle with water. Drop the straw in and put on the lid. Squeeze the bottle.

Squeeze the bottle

What happens to the straw?

4 When you squeeze the sides of the bottle, your straw sinks, like a fish diving to the bottom. When you let go, it floats back up again.

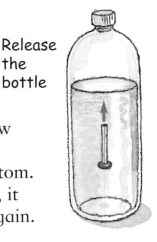

Release the bottle

Sleepless shark

A shark looks fierce with its mouth wide open, but it may only be breathing! As it swims forwards, water flows into its mouth and out through its gills. Oxygen goes into its blood to keep its body working. If the shark stops moving forwards, it cannot get enough oxygen and it drowns.

WOW!

Water in through the mouth

Water out through the gills

Water plants help to make oxygen for fish.

Can pets talk to us?

How does your pet tell you that it wants to be fed? Does it make a noise, or let you know in some other way? Animals do not have conversations, but they can give each other, and us, very clear messages. The sounds they make and their silent signals are called body language. They show us what a pet is thinking or feeling. If we know what to look for, we can tell whether animals are well and happy or are feeling sad and unwell.

What does a cat say if you step on its tail?

Miaa-OW!

Sending signals

A sad dog

A dog with its tail between its legs is miserable, while a happy dog wags its tail. A cat swishes its tail to show that it is cross, and holds its tail upright when it is contented.

Some animals use ultrasonic squeaks which we cannot hear, and leave scent messages that we cannot smell.

A cross cat

A dog sniffing scent messages.

A parrot does not make sounds in the same way that we do.

Pieces of eight!

A 'talking' bird mimics sounds that it has heard. It doesn't actually understand what it is saying.

See for yourself!

1 Watch a dog when it is very pleased to see someone. It wags its tail and rolls over on its back to have its tummy tickled.

2 When a cat is pleased to see you, it rubs itself against your legs and purrs loudly. It wants you to stroke it.

3 But watch it when it is scared by a dog. It arches its back, fluffs out its fur and tries to look big and fierce.

4 Listen to the sounds pigeons and doves make. They coo to each other to show they care. They even coo to their eggs.

Long-distance call!

WOW!

Animals like to guard their territory and keep away intruders. Lions can roar very loudly to warn off rival lions. They can be heard as far away as eight kilometres.

Learn to understand your pet.

What can my dog hear?

A dog has very good hearing. The ear flaps on its head collect sound, and send it down to the eardrums inside. The eardrums are round patches of skin, which vibrate when sound reaches them through the air. Deeper still, the sound vibrations reach the *inner ear* which sends messages to the brain. If you look at a frog, you can actually see what eardrums look like – they are on either side of its head.

What does your dog like to listen to?

His eardrums!

Sound sensations

You can see the eardrum on a frog, but a dog's eardrum, like yours, is hidden inside its head. Behind that is the inner ear. Different parts of the inner ear pick up high, medium and low sounds.

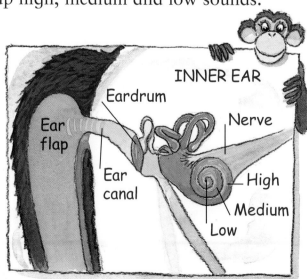

INNER EAR

Eardrum

Ear flap

Nerve

Ear canal

High

Medium

Low

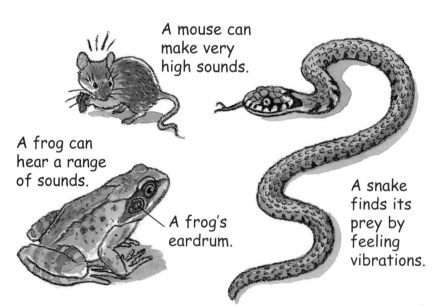

A mouse can make very high sounds.

A frog can hear a range of sounds.

A frog's eardrum.

A snake finds its prey by feeling vibrations.

Many small mammals, such as mice and bats, use ultrasound – very high sounds which humans cannot hear. Dogs can hear ultrasound too.

Snakes and fish are deaf, but their bodies can feel even the slightest vibrations coming through the ground or water.

See for yourself!

1 Imagine what it would be like to be a snake. You could feel vibrations coming through the air. Put your hands on a loudspeaker when music is playing. Can you feel the beat?

Speaker

2 Wrap some thin paper round a comb. It makes a simple musical instrument.

Comb

3 Pout your lips forwards and put the comb against them. Now make a tooting noise, so that the paper vibrates. Try to toot a tune. The vibrations will tickle your lips.

WOW! Bouncing sound!

Bats in the air use *echolocation* to catch moths. Dolphins in the sea also use echolocation to find shoals of fish. The bats bounce sounds off objects and wait for the echoes to come back. This tells them how far away their next meal is, and how fast they have to go to catch it.

Do not upset fish or reptiles by tapping on their tanks.

Do not disturb!

Why is my hamster soft?

Like most *mammals*, hamsters are covered in hair. Their hair feels soft because they are fine and short and can bend easily when you touch them. Touching an animal with longer, coarser hair, such as a shaggy dog, feels different. Chicks are covered in fine, soft feathers called *down*. Soft, fluffy animals are usually *warm-blooded*. Their fluff traps air next to their bodies, acting as *insulation* and keeping them warm.

Which side of a hamster has the most fur?

The outside!

Chilly creatures

Earthworms are *cold-blooded*. They don't have a furry covering because they breathe through their skin.

A worm has no fluff to keep it warm.

Terrapins have shells and scaly skin.

Some insects look fluffy though they are not warm-blooded. Take care! They are not as cuddly as they look.

Bees may sting.

Birds have feathers, which are like branched hairs.

Reptiles can't be fluffy because they are also cold-blooded creatures. They need the sunshine on their scaly skin to warm themselves up.

Some caterpillars are poisonous. Do not touch!

See for yourself!

1 Does everything that looks soft feel the same? Pick two toys that look fluffy and two toys that look smooth.

Velvet teddy

Rubber ball

Wooden train

Wooden mouse

Cotton block

Plastic duck

2 Ask someone to put one of the toys in a bag. Put your hand in the bag and see if your fingers can tell whether it is a smooth or fluffy toy. Can you also feel what it is from its shape and size?

Bag

3 Compare the fluffy toys and the smooth toys. Which ones feel warmer to the touch? Do any of them feel cold?

Prickly Hair

WOW!

Quill

A porcupine is covered with coarse hair and sharp quills.

If lots of long hairs are stuck together, they can be really hard and spiky, not soft and fluffy. A porcupine's quills are hairs, but it is definitely not cuddly! The animal uses its quills to protect itself from its enemies.

Never cuddle animals you don't know.

15

How does my rabbit hop?

What happens if you make a rabbit angry?

It goes hopping mad!

If you watch a rabbit, you will see that it moves in a different way to a cat or dog – it hops. This is because its back legs are longer than its front legs. Strong leg muscles push its hind feet back against the ground, and this *force* shoots its body forwards. Its front feet go to the ground to balance it as it lands. When a rabbit is jumping, its four feet are in the air.

What can hop?

Frogs can make large leaps, but they cannot bounce along like a rabbit.

Frog

A rabbit's legs store energy for the next hop.

Rabbit

The wallaby's tail helps it to balance as it leaps along.

Dot

Wallabies and kangaroos have long hind legs, but they can hop without using their front legs. They balance themselves with their tails.

Archie

An elephant has front and back legs the same length, so it cannot hop. When an elephant walks it lifts only one foot off the ground at a time.

16

See for yourself!

1 Watch animals move and try to copy them. It is hard because we have the wrong arms and legs. Try being a snake and wriggle along the floor without using your arms and legs at all.

Marie being a snake

2 Try lifting yourself off the floor like a lizard or a crocodile, with your arms and legs bent and sticking out to the side. It is very tiring for your muscles.

Marie being a crocodile

3 Straighten your arms and legs underneath you, like a horse or elephant. Your arms are too short, so you may fall on your face!

Marie being a horse

4 It is easier if you bend your legs, let your arms hang down and walk like a chimpanzee. Or you can bend your legs and hop like a frog or rabbit.

Marie being a frog

WOW!

High jumps!

A flea can jump a hundred times its own body height. It stores energy in special pads where its legs join its body. This stored energy is released as the flea jumps, giving extra power to push it through the air.

Can you play hop scotch?

Can my cat see in the dark?

A cat can see well both in daylight and at night, but no animal can see if it is totally dark. An animal needs light to reach the *retina* at the back of its eyes to enable it to see. The retina sends a message to the *brain*, which works out what the eye has seen. *Nocturnal* animals come out at night, and have special eyes that make the most of what light there is. They also use other senses, like touch, to help them find their way.

What kind of eyes make driving safer?

Cats' eyes!

Night sight

A cat's *pupils* are narrow slits in bright sunshine, but open wider to let in more light when it starts to get dark.

Behind a cat's retina is a layer that reflects light. This helps them to see better in dim light. It makes their eyes 'light up' if you shine a torch in them.

Some nocturnal animals, such as bushbabies, have very big eyes to help them see in dim light.

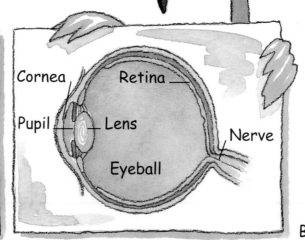

Pupil — Daytime

Pupil — Night-time

Cornea
Pupil
Retina
Lens
Nerve
Eyeball

Bushbaby

See for yourself!

1 Large glass marbles are the same shape as eyeballs but, unlike eyes, they let in light from all sides.

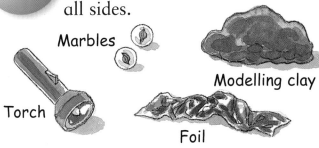

Marbles

Modelling clay

Torch

Foil

2 Make a face from modelling clay, and push in two marbles for eyes. If you shine a torch at them, they will look quite dull.

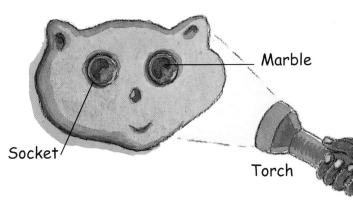

Marble

Socket

Torch

3 Now, line the eye sockets with shiny foil before you push in the eyes. They will shine like cats' eyes when you turn your torch on them.

Foil

Torch

WOW!

Hot on the trail!

At night, some snakes hunt small rodents. Near their nostrils are little heat-sensitive pits that pick up the body heat coming from their warm-blooded prey. They do not need to see the prey with their eyes.

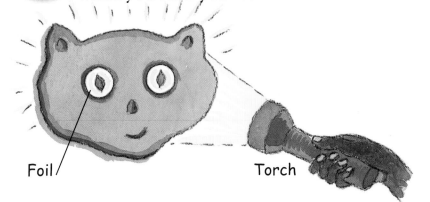

Be careful in the dark - don't trip over things!

How does my budgie keep clean?

What do you give a dirty budgie?

Beauty tweetment!

Animals need to keep their skin, fur or feathers in good condition to prevent disease. Many spend a lot of time cleaning themselves to remove the little creatures called *parasites* which live on their bodies. Some pets need help from their owners to brush out long, tangled fur. Birds, however, clean their feathers with their beaks – a process called *preening*. Some birds bathe while swimming, others wet their feathers in puddles or bird baths. If no water is available, many birds will take a dust bath.

See for yourself!

1 Collect some of the feathers that fall out of your bird's cage, or look out for them in parks or gardens.

2 Contour feathers are smooth, and give the bird a streamlined surface. Downy feathers, which keep the bird warm, have a thinner shaft and are fluffy.

Vane (flat area)

Barbs hook together to make the vane

Thick shaft down the middle

Contour feather

Thin shaft

Fluffy branches

Downy feather

Good grooming

A bird has a long neck, so that it can reach the preen gland under its tail. It spreads oil from its gland onto its feathers to make them *waterproof*.

Birds use their beaks to press together and refasten the hooks of the barbs in their feathers. This keeps them tidy.

Cats and dogs use their front *incisor teeth* to comb their fur and remove the dirt and tangles. A dog nibbles its fur with its teeth and licks it clean with its wet tongue.

A cat also uses its rough tongue to wash itself. The tongue's surface is covered with tiny hooks that groom the fur – working like a brush and comb.

Flying pens

WOW!

Large wing feathers from geese were once used to make quill pens. The end of the hollow shaft was sliced off and shaped into a pointed tip, which was then dipped in ink for writing.

Always be gentle with your pet!

21

Why is a snake scaly?

Why do snakes make bad musicians?

Because they keep losing their scales!

Have you ever wondered why a snake's skin is covered with *scales*? Like other animals, a snake's body is made mainly of water, and would soon dry out in the air if it didn't have a waterproof layer on the outside. Water is lost from the surface of an animal's body by *evaporation*. If an animal loses too much water, it will die. The waterproof scales that cover a snake's body help to keep in water, and stop it from drying out. They also protect the snake as it slithers over rough ground.

Skin types

Scales

Scales protect the skin of fish from drying out in salty seawater. They also prevent fish from getting waterlogged in freshwater.

Mammals, such as mice, have an outer layer of oily skin under their fur to keep them waterproof.

Mice

Animals that don't have waterproof skins must live in damp places. For example, earthworms and frogs have soft, moist skins that dry out quickly in air.

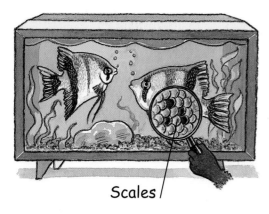

Frog

Earthworms

22

See for yourself!

1 Draw the outline of a fish or a snake on a piece of card.

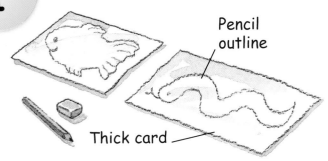

Pencil outline

Thick card

2 Cut out scales from pieces of coloured paper, or use some coloured stickers.

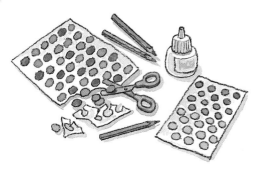

3 Starting at the tail end, stick on overlapping scales to cover the shape you have drawn.

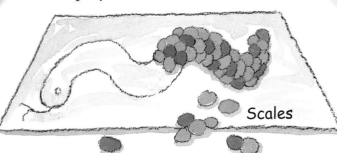

Scales

4 If you use pieces of modelling clay, you can make your animal armour-plated.

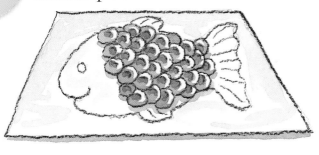

Modelling clay

WOW!

Armour-plated!

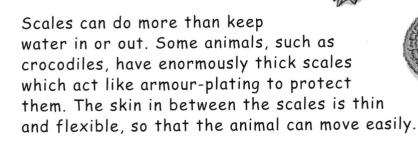

Never touch an animal in the wild!

Scales can do more than keep water in or out. Some animals, such as crocodiles, have enormously thick scales which act like armour-plating to protect them. The skin in between the scales is thin and flexible, so that the animal can move easily.

Why is my mouse brown?

The colour of an animal's fur or feathers helps to protect it. Sunlight is harmful as it contains ultraviolet light which can cause sunburn. An animal's colour acts like a sunblock, preventing the skin from burning. The colour of an animal's skin, hair, fur and feathers comes from *melanin*. Black or brown animals produce a lot of melanin, and are more protected from sunlight than creatures with lighter-coloured bodies. An animal's colour also blends it into its surroundings, helping it to hide. This is called *camouflage*.

Eeeek!

When is it bad luck to see a black cat?

When you're a mouse!

Eye colours

The coloured part of the eye is called the *iris*. If it is brown, it contains a lot of melanin. This protects the eye from bright sunlight.

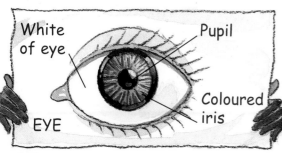

White of eye

Pupil

Coloured iris

EYE

Green iris

Eyes with less melanin are blue, green or even yellow.

People and animals with no melanin at all are called albinos. They have white hair and skin, and pink eyes, and need to stay out of the sun.

24

See for yourself!

1 Look at your family and pets. Make drawings of their eyes. How many different colours can you see?

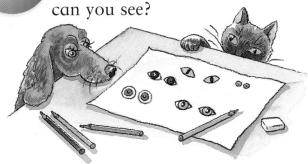

2 Can you find hairs and feathers which have fallen out round the house? Dark hairs are hard to see on dark furniture and clothes.

Hair

3 Paint and cut out an animal that has several colours in its coat. Paint a background in the same colours. If you cannot easily see the animal against the background, it is camouflaged.

Fine feathers

WOW!

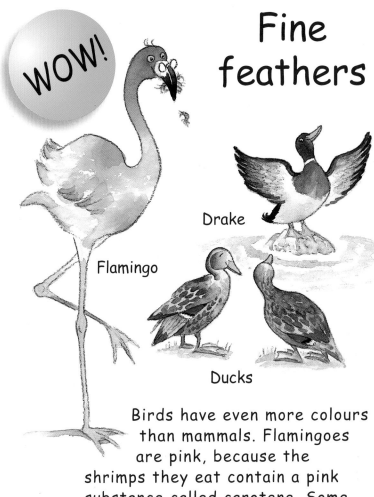

Flamingo

Drake

Ducks

Birds have even more colours than mammals. Flamingoes are pink, because the shrimps they eat contain a pink substance called carotene. Some birds have tiny hollow 'bubbles' in their feathers which *refract* or split up light to give rainbow colours. Female birds choose the males with the brightest colours.

Always protect your skin – it can burn easily.

What does my guinea pig eat?

What do you call a dull guinea pig?

A herbi-bore!

A guinea pig spends most of its time nibbling grass. This gives it the energy and nutrients it needs to live. To look after a pet properly, you must know what it should eat and how often.

Guinea pigs eat plants because they are *herbivores*. Their wild relatives in South America eat grass, roots and shoots. If pet guinea pigs are kept indoors and cannot have fresh grass, they will eat hay, which is dried grass and mixtures of seed.

Pets' menu

If animals are kept as pets, they must have the right food. Like guinea pigs, rabbits and gerbils are herbivores, and so are stick insects.

Animals, like this chameleon, which need to eat lots of live, wriggly insects are called *insectivores*.

In the wild, *carnivores* eat other animals. Everything gets eaten, even plants in the stomachs of their prey. Tinned pet food has to contain the balance of nutrients a dog needs.

Menu — Grass — Fresh hay

Menu — Nuts & seeds

Menu — Privet — Brambles

Menu — Crickets

Menu — Meat

See for yourself!

1 Animals know what they like. Try putting a dish of cat food and a pile of hay in front of a guinea pig. It will eat the hay because it is a herbivore.

Cat food · Hay

2 Do the same with a cat and it will turn up its nose at the hay. Cats eat meat. They are carnivores.

Hay

Cat food

3 Put a dish of cat food in front of a dog. It will eat it. It is a carnivore too – and it cannot read labels.

Cat food

4 Do mice and rats really like cheese? Try it and see, but only give them a little. Too much could be bad for them and make them smelly.

Mouse · Rat

Chubby cheeks!

WOW!

Hamsters have special pouches in their cheeks, so that if there is plenty of food, they can collect it and carry it away to store it. A tiny hamster can fit seeds as large as acorns snugly in its cheeks.

Guinea pigs need food containing vitamin C.

Why does my dog play?

Have you watched a puppy chase a ball or pounce on its mother's tail? In the wild, most grown-up animals don't play. They are too busy just staying alive. When baby animals play they are practising the skills they will need when they grow up. Young carnivores pretend to hunt, and have play fights to work out which one is boss. Animals, such as dogs, which we keep as pets, often stay playful even when they are grown-up.

Why does a dog chase its tail?

To make both ends meet!

Fun and games

Look out for some of the things different animals do to amuse themselves. Dogs enjoy chasing sticks and bringing them back.

A budgie on its own will play with its mirror.

Lambs and kids run about in the fields, and play 'I'm the king of the castle'.

Intelligent animals, such as monkeys, need plenty of things to do. Otherwise they get bored.

See for yourself!

1 Pets do not need expensive toys. Tie a folded paper 'butterfly' to a piece of string, and trail it in front of a cat. It will be quite happy to pounce on it.

2 Hold the butterfly up above the cat's head. It will reach up and bat it with its paws.

3 Fill up a little cloth bag with the herb called catnip and your cat will play with it for hours.

Cloth mouse

Cloth bag

Catnip

Tie up the end.

4 Wash out an empty plastic milk container for your dog. He will chase it if you throw it – and play tug-of-war.

Milk container

Play school!

WOW!

Porpoises and dolphins are the only wild animals that actually choose to play with humans. They follow boats and sometimes approach swimmers near the beach.

Pets need peace and quiet as well as playtimes!

Pets quiz

1 Where does a cat make purring sounds?
 a) In its throat
 b) In its tail
 c) In its tummy

2 What does a hamster's soft fur do?
 a) It helps it to keep warm
 b) It helps it to breathe
 c) It helps it to keep dry

3 What does a bird use to clean itself?
 a) Its beak
 b) Its tongue
 c) Its teeth

4 What does a fish use to float upwards in water?
 a) Its gills
 b) Its scales
 c) Its swim bladder

5 When does a dog put its tail between its legs?
 a) When it is miserable
 b) When it is happy
 c) When it is angry

6 Which pair of legs is longer in a rabbit?
 a) The back legs
 b) The front legs
 c) Neither - they are the same

7 Which part of the cat's eye gets larger at night?
 a) The retina
 b) The iris
 c) The pupil

8 What is a snake's body covered with?
 a) Fur
 b) Feathers
 c) Scales

9 What is an animal with white hair and pink eyes called?
 a) A palomino
 b) An albino
 c) A pigment

10 What is the name given to an animal that only eats plants?
 a) A carnivore
 b) A herbivore
 c) An insectivore

Answers on page 32

Glossary

Brain
The organ inside the skull that receives information from the body and tells it what to do.

Camouflage
Colouring or shape that helps to hide an object.

Carnivores
Animals that catch and eat other animals, or eat those killed by others.

Cold-blooded
Animals that cannot make their own body heat. They take their heat from their surroundings.

Down
Small, soft, fluffy feathers that keep birds warm.

Echolocation
The system used by bats and dolphins to find their way in the dark.

Energy
The ability to do work or make something happen.

Evaporation
When water turns from being visible liquid to invisible water vapour.

Fins
Parts of the body of a fish that help the fish to swim, steer and balance.

Force
A push or pull which can change something's movement or shape.

Gills
Delicate parts, behind a fish's head, used for absorbing oxygen from the water into its blood.

Herbivores
Animals that eat only plant material.

Incisor teeth
Sharp teeth at the front of the mouth, used for biting and nibbling.

Inner ear
Part of the ear, protected by bone, sensitive to sound vibrations and head movements.

Insectivore
Animals that eat insects, worms and other small invertebrates.

Insulation
A material used to slow down or stop the movement of heat.

Iris
The coloured part at the front of the eye, which controls how much light enters the eye.

Mammals
Air-breathing, hair-covered, bony animals, which can make their own body heat.

Melanin
The pigment in the skin of animals, in all shades from yellowish to black, that protects against ultraviolet light.

Nocturnal
Awake and active during the night.

Parasites
Small animals that live and feed on a larger animal, either inside it or on its skin.

Preening
When a bird uses its beak to comb its feathers into place and to make them waterproof with oil from its preen gland.

Pupils
The round holes or slits in the centre of the iris, through which light enters the eye.

Refract
To alter the direction in which light is travelling. This can make something look as though it has changed size or colour.

Retina
The layer at the back of the eye, which sends messages to the brain when light falls on it.

Scales
Waterproof plates, usually thin and transparent, that form a layer over the skin of reptiles and bony fishes.

Swim bladder
A long thin bag, just under a fish's backbone, which can be filled with air to help it float.

Vocal cords
Folds in the lining of the voice box vibrated by the breath to produce the voice.

Warm-blooded
Mammals and birds whose bodies are warmed by energy released from food.

Waterproof
Will not let water pass through or stick to it.

Index

Answers to the Pets quiz on page 30
1 In its throat. **2** It helps it to keep warm.
3 Its beak. **4** Its swim bladder. **5** When it is miserable. **6** The back legs. **7** The pupil.
8 Scales. **9** An albino. **10** A herbivore.